80 Years of Pets Galore

JUNE WIEHE

Cedar Creek Publishing
Bremo Bluff, Virginia
www.cedarcreekauthors.com

*Cover photos: (Front) June with "Cindy"
(Back) June, age 10, with "Fluffy"
and June in garden with "Chipper"*

*Title page photo: June, age 7, with
her neighbor's dog, "Queenie"*

*Dedication page photo: June (on right) with
her parents and "Sandy" and "Pal"*

Printed in the United States of America

Library of Congress Control Number 2010942612

ISBN 978-0-9659419-4-5

To my parents
Ruth and Ernst Wiehe
who also had a
passion for animals

"King" on my lap

Acknowledgments

This book would not have come to fruition were it not for Linda Layne, my wonderful friend, editor, and publisher and her daughter, Ashley. Because of macular degeneration, the text was written in very poor long hand which Ashley miraculously was able to interpret and type. Then Linda had the proofs printed in huge type to make it easy for me.

This book came to be because so many friends said I should write the stories I told them of my pets' antics. Many thanks to all.

JUNE WIEHE

Me holding "Fluffy"

Chapter One

People who love animals tend to want to share stories about them and I am no exception. I have had many pets in my long life and it would be a pleasure to share some of the antics and adventures with you.

My first pets were goldfish, canaries, and rabbits. I was eight years old when I got my first kitten - a beautiful tabby - I appropriately called "Kitty."* She was the runt of the litter but queen of all she surveyed! She was boss of the neighborhood.

Somehow, Kitty knew the exact boundaries of our property. A dog could walk the sidewalk without challenge, but let him put one paw on "her" property and she was after him like a shot. I remember one evening when we were all sitting

* Unfortunately, no photos exist of "Kitty."

in the front yard – Kitty included. A German shepherd came along and innocently stepped into the yard. Kitty gave a banshee yell and charged him in screaming fury. The dog took off up the street "k-y-y-ing" for all he was worth – the tiny cat right behind his tail, screaming her insults as loud as she could. We were three doors from the corner. She chased him the other way, all the way, off the block. It was so funny to see people running out of their houses to see who was being killed! The sight of a tiny cat chasing a big dog had everyone roaring with laughter. Especially when Kitty came strutting down the street waving her tail like a banner, proud as a peacock, accepting her applause as only a royal queen could do.

When our car was parked in the yard, she loved to be under it and wait for an imposter. One day it was a Saint Bernard! Her charge with the banshee scream was all she needed; he never waited to see what was after him!

She also enjoyed sitting on the front stoop where she greeted anyone who came – except anyone in what she considered a uniform! Back in the 30's during the Depression, companies would hire people to walk neighborhoods to deliver samples of new products (forerunners of commercials). Usually they wore some sort of uniform. Unfortunately for us, if Kitty was on guard, we didn't get the sample unless we were quick to hear her battle cry. Even the bravest of men would be turned away with her greeting of an arched back, hisses and screams!

There were many children on our block in a range of ages, and Kitty was considered "one of us." She enjoyed being the center of attention, even dressed up in doll clothes and being pushed about in a baby buggy! Then came the day she had five little kittens in a comfortable bed by the cellar steps. All the children were welcome to come and admire her brood – but beware a stranger!

Water and gas meters were in the cellar back then, so you left the door open for the meter men to come in unannounced and read them. Kitty and her family were on one side of the cellar steps – the meters on the other.

One day, we heard the cellar door open and my mother and I, and Grandma (who lived with us), all yelled "Kitty" at the same time. Grandma was closest to the cellar steps and was halfway down when Kitty launched herself at the meter man passing on the other side of the steps. None of us could say just how she did it, but Grandma caught Kitty in midair and saved the meter man a scratched face.

After that episode – and Kitty's watchdog tendencies – Mother was able to convince me to keep one of the male kittens and send Kitty and the rest to our neighbor's farm. One of my girl friends took a black kitten, and I picked a gray one I named, "Fluffy," because he had such great, dense fur.

My girl friend named her kitten "Blackie" (what else?), and he and Fluffy were great friends.

My friend and I with our cats "Blackie" and "Fluffy."

Fluffy in the tree with me on the watch

Fluffy was the opposite of his mother. He was gentle and laid back – friends with everyone. One thing I must mention is that with Kitty and Fluffy, we also had a canary named "Billy" and never had any problems. From kittenhood on they learned the house rules – no jumping up on tables or counters, and absolutely no bird bothering!

Neither cat ever bothered Billy or even the wild birds outside. We could go out for the day, leaving cat and bird in the house together, and our trust was never violated. Actually, we never gave it much thought. We taught them how to behave – and they did! A few shocked "No's" were all they ever needed.

Fluffy was about a year old when my father was transferred to New York. We lived on Long Island. Fluffy stayed with Blackie until we were settled. Then my grandfather made a big crate and shipped him to New York. The trip traumatized poor Fluffy so badly that he never recovered. For over a week I walked him outside with a harness to accustom him to the area, but the first time we let him out on his own, he disappeared, never to be seen again. I was devastated. In Ohio, there had been large yards and quiet streets. On Long Island, the yards were postage stamps and we lived on a main street with buses. We did not voluntarily get another cat – but we did get another canary.

One day, however, another kitty wandered in. She stayed long enough to have a litter of kittens. Fearing the road, we had a friend take her and her kittens to the racetrack where she was welcomed with open arms. A few weeks later, she turned up on our doorstep. She had weaned her kittens and returned to the home she wanted.

Me with my neighbor, Bob, and the wanderer kitty and her kittens

It was not a long journey, as some cats have made, it was a matter of only two or three miles. She had been taken in a closed box and we thought she would stay with her kittens. Naturally, we could not turn her away after that! Unfortunately, her stay was short. A few months later, she crossed the road and a car ended her life. It took another bite out of my heart because, each time a loved pet goes a bit of you goes, too, but precious memories remain.

Mama kitty came back briefly

Whiskers - King of the Neighborhood

Chapter Two

A few months later, yet another cat wandered in! The most strikingly handsome cat I have ever known. His twenty-pound body was adorned in glossy black fur with almost perfect white accents. He was always dressed in "evening clothes." A tuxedo?

He had gorgeous emerald green eyes that sparkled with intelligence, but it was the outstanding white whiskers sprouting from his jet-black face that earned him the name "Whiskers!" (What else?)

He was a huge animal that carried his weight like a trained boxer. The photos do not do justice to his actual size. I was even surprised myself at his size after being gone for a year.

The vet estimated his age was five years, and for months after he came, his actions nearly broke our hearts. He was still hoping to find a master he had obviously loved. It was during World War

II, so we guessed his master had to go to war and left him behind. When someone went by whistling, Whiskers would run to the glass door and look out expectantly - but it was never who he hoped it was and he would plod slowly back to his chair and curl up so dejected. Different, apparently remembered sounds, would animate him until he realized it was not the one he missed.

Whiskers was first and foremost a one-family cat and would have nothing to do with strangers. If we had company and he was sleeping in his private chair, he would endure a certain amount of petting, but if it continued, he would jump off and go in the cellar until the callers left. He never ran away – he would just jump off in unhurried dignity, with pride written all over his body.

To strangers, Whiskers was a proud aristocrat. He reserved his love and attention solely for us. If we scolded him or laughed at his clumsy attempts to play, he would go in the cellar and sulk until his wounded vanity was assuaged by the dark loneliness. However, his sojourn could be shortened if someone went down and assured him all was forgiven.

Whiskers strutting through snow

Whiskers did not care to be held. A chin rubbing and pat on the head sufficed to keep him happy. If we told him he was a good cat, he was in cat heaven. His knowledge of the human vocabulary was astounding. Just pointing to an object centered his attention on it immediately. A piece of dropped food that he missed would get his instant attention if we pointed at it. Even if we were across the room from an object, Whiskers would look at the pointing finger and follow the direction it pointed. If he missed the object of his search, he would look back for assurance and look again where we were pointing. It never took more than two tries for him to find it.

Whiskers in his perfect sit up to beg

A spoken, "Over there, Whiskers," and a wave of the hand in the general direction held a volume of meaning to him! He was a smart cat!

When he decided we were "his family" he became very possessive. It was "his yard" and "his house," and he resented any one "horning" on "his property!"

When friends visited us and brought their dog, Whiskers was always ready to go on the offensive! He had to be locked in the cellar to save the dog from a scratched nose! Penned up, he would sit at the door and grumble about what he'd do to that dog if he could!

When the company had gone and Whiskers was let out, he went over the whole house minutely to learn where the dog had been. In addition, he could not be dissuaded before his tour of duty was completed to his satisfaction!

Whiskers was so highly intelligent he learned tricks readily. Sitting up to beg came hardest because he was like a caged tiger at feeding time. He would stand on his hind legs reaching up for food. It took patience and love but he finally learned the quickest way to get his food was just

Whiskers jumping through my arms

to sit up on his hind legs – not stand up! One of the photos shows him doing this to perfection.

Next, I taught him to shake paw. He liked this so much; he often sat waving his paw at us in an invitation to shake it! He also liked rolling over on command. Next came jumping through my circled arms or over a stick.

His intelligence was in evidence the day he came home in big trouble. That day he came in with sticky tar stuck to the hair and pads of his feet. For an hour he laid on the floor and let me work on getting it off, which proved to be a hard, painful operation. It hurt and he growled and rumbled but he never moved or tried to jerk a paw away. He knew perfectly well he needed help and that I was giving it – so he endured – but not in silence!

I graduated from high school and went back to Kentucky to be with my grandmother. All our relatives lived in Kentucky and Ohio and I had missed them. Whiskers stayed with my parents on Long Island. I got a job and enjoyed the home territory where we could get butter and meat with coupons and there was no blackout. You knew you were in a war on Long Island. There were air raids,

Me during my graduation year

constant blackouts, and rationed food almost impossible to get – coupons or not.

A year later, my folks were forced to move from the rented house because the owners wanted to move back in. The time they had finding another place is a story in itself. Suffice it to say, they had to buy a house in New Jersey.

I returned to help them move. I had been away for a year and I wondered if Whiskers would remember me as well as he remembered his former master. He met me at the door and looked at me with unfathomable eyes. When I said, "Whiskers, don't you know me?" he began to sniff my legs.

When I sat down in the middle of the kitchen floor, Whiskers crawled into my lap as if he had found what he wanted and began to purr like an outboard motor! Whiskers was not a lap cat but it was obvious he had really missed me and was overjoyed to have me back!

Even though a year had passed, his nose had told him his eyes had not deceived him. Whiskers did not like strangers. He had never even made up with our neighbors he saw every day. Yet, he immediately crawled into my lap and began kneading with his paws like a kitten. He remembered.

His greeting was so overwhelming I had to cry. It made me remember how he had missed his first master and grieved for him. I did worry, though, about the move. Would I lose him as we had lost Fluffy?

I need not have worried. Whiskers was family oriented and we had moved to the country with miles of fields and woods around us. Whiskers was a city cat – used to traffic and 40 x 100 town lots. Now with acres of fields and woods all around, Whiskers was like a child with a new toy.

He would race from one end to the other then climb the trees in one grand rush only to leap down and pant after each exertion. It was probably the most exercise he had ever done in his life but he gloried in it.

Needless to say, Whiskers took to the new life like a duck to water and I found him a new and better pal – as good and companionable as a dog. We took long walks through the wild countryside – Whiskers following like a dog.

When he tired, he would sit down and if I did not wait for him, he'd howl! One day I kept going until I was well out of sight. Suddenly, missing him and worrying he might get lost; I stopped and looked around and saw an amazing sight. Coming round a bend in the trail was Whiskers – nose to the ground following my scent like a bloodhound. When I called him, he trotted up with what I could only interpret as a grin on his face. His look was as plain as words, "Fooled you, didn't I? You can't lose me!" And he laughed with that expressive tail.

This became a favorite game and I could never fool him no matter how devious I tried to mix up my trail.

Whiskers was my watchdog and protector as well as companion and I never worried with him at my heels. He was a good detector and warned me of anything in the immediate vicinity. He would freeze into position and I'd keep still until I found the cause of his attention. Usually it was a rabbit or chipmunk, but if it were a dog, a low growl would let me know. I have no doubt he would have given battle to anything that threatened us because he was a fighter – and my pal. Behind Whiskers' emerald eyes were shadows of his brothers under the skin who roam free in the wild - panthers, leopards, tigers, and lions.

Whiskers

Unfortunately, we had only several months of mutual bliss. Being city raised we had never been exposed to hunting seasons. Whiskers was shot and killed next to a "No Hunting" sign. Through terrible tears, I wrote Whisker's final epitaph:

⚞ IN MEMORY OF WHISKERS ⚟

My cat did not come home last night-
He was some hunter's "game."
I called and called into the night
But, all my calls were in vain.

My cat did not come home to me
Some hunter out for "sport"
Had sent a bullet gleefully
For him there is no court.

I do not know who fired the shot
Perhaps it's better so
Whoever left him in the lot
Is not a man to know.

For who could shoot a cat like that
Is of the lowest type
For how'd he know what meant that cat
To someone not in sight?

That Whiskers cat was my dear pet
And oh! I loved him so
And some good "sporting hunter" left
The life blood from him flow

Oh how I long to see him come
With springy trot so free
When at my call he'd start to run
To hurry up to me

But someone took a "sporting" shot
And I am lonely now
No Whiskers comes to call me out
He made his final bow.

My cat did not come home last night
He'll never come again
The dawn will never bring him light
Because of "sporting" men!

Chapter Three

A few months after losing Whiskers, we were having a raging blizzard when our neighbor called. He'd found a stray kitten huddled against his cellar window trying to escape the storm. Would we want it?

No! We did not want it – Whiskers' death was still too close. We wanted no more heartbreaks like that – but we'd take a look. (Famous last words!)

Despite the storm, our neighbor brought him over and one look was all it took! We fell like a ton of bricks for the sweet-faced little kitten that looked to be part Persian – so heavy was his fur. He had fluffy orange stripes and the most appealing face that yearned for love.

However, when we put him down, we learned he was a very sick little pussy. He hobbled pitifully on three legs. His right foreleg seemed to be broken near the shoulder. He was also sick

Tinker in his summer coat

internally with terrible diarrhea. Unfortunately, we were snowed in with four feet of that beautiful white stuff called snow. It was impossible to get out to take him to a vet. So we did all we could with home doctoring.

We made him a bed in the kitchen and dosed him with Pepto-Bismol but we quickly learned all he wanted was love! He craved affection more than food and you can be sure he received it! We named him "Tinker" because it seemed to fit.

For weeks, he was too sick to do much but eat and sleep, but as he recovered, he tried to play. On three legs, it was not so easy, but he gradually got used to the handicap and then the fun began! He learned to get around better on three legs than most cats on four.

He was a regular crackerjack! He loved to make us laugh! The more we laughed, the better he liked it and the crazier he'd get! He'd race through the house like a dozen dogs were on his tail and rugs would go flying in every direction! Upstairs and downstairs sliding on the kitchen linoleum and all you could do was get out of his way!

His favorite trick was running full tilt into the

Tinker playing as a kitten

kitchen and putting on the brakes to slide into whatever was in his way, then taking off again with a mad scramble of paws going nowhere fast! And, he did this all on just three legs!

For a long while we were all afraid we had a permanent three-legged cat but gradually he began to use the injured leg and then the fun really began! If we thought he was a whiz before, now he traveled on jet fuel! He adored playing and showing off to an audience. Unlike most cats who hate to have anyone laugh at them, Tinker loved to hear people laugh and he went to great lengths just to gain that laughter.

He was the biggest show-off there ever was. Unlike Whiskers who was highly insulted if laughed at, Tinker loved to make people laugh. He loved an audience and expected applause. Like Whiskers, he learned all sorts of tricks but games are what he loved the most. One favorite was hide and seek – and don't think he didn't know what that meant! The house was not much of a challenge – closets for me and behind furniture for him was about all we could manage, but out of doors he was as good a tracker as Whiskers.

No cat ever loved a practical joke more than Tinker did and he could dish them out as well as take them. One game, which started out as a practical joke, I wished I hadn't started . . .

One day I saw him strolling into the living room and I hid behind a chair. As he passed by I jumped out at him and he leaped into the air and took off. Of course, that made me roar with laughter and taught him that I really had caught him unaware that time!

A short time later, I passed that chair and Tinker leaped out at me with about the same result he'd given. Well, that became his favorite past time from then on. He would hide and leap at anyone who passed by, loving the screams and jumps we gave! It wasn't long before he improved on it – from his standpoint anyway! He'd jump out and grab a leg! Never any claws – just a quick grab and release! Next came a gentle nip with the grab!

He never forgot this game and we never knew when he'd spring it on one of us. Sometimes it would be days without a Tinker "attack." Other times he'd have everyone yelling, "Tinker! Cut that out!"

Tinker - battle pose

Another thing Tinker loved was at least three bowls of food at once. One had to be milk. Usually one was cat food; the other was some kind of "human" food. Tinker would check each one out then happily settle down. He would move from one to another – back and forth until each was empty.

Lucky

The following year, Dad came home with a small black kitten he'd found crying in the woods when he took a walk. Someone had obviously dumped it – it was starving and cold, and scared to death. Tinker took to it at once, grooming and loving it! There

Tinker and Lucky sleeping in "their" chair

was no other name we could give the kitten but "Lucky" - so lucky Dad had taken the walk in the right place at the right time!

I've heard tomcats will often kill kittens, but I've never seen anything but love shown as these true stories will tell as I write on.

Tinker and Lucky became the best of pals. They ate, played, and slept together. For a long while, Lucky was strictly a house cat and when Tinker would come in from his outside excursions he'd let out an, "I'm home — Where are you?" Sometimes Lucky would be in the cellar and Lucky would come running. Their greetings to each other would be as though they had been parted for weeks!

Sadly, after Lucky began his outside journeys, instead of going to the back where there was nothing but woods and fields, one day he went to the front where there was a major highway some 500 feet away. He was killed, and as always, part of our hearts died with him. But not only ours, Tinker's as well.

For weeks after we lost Lucky, we were afraid we'd lose Tinker to a broken heart. He went around the house crying, searching for his pal. When he would come in from outside he'd dash to the cellar door and call and call. When Lucky didn't appear - he'd plod dejectedly to the chair they had always shared and curl up. He grieved for Lucky and was never the same clown he'd been before. He never forgot and each time he came in the house he'd go to the cellar steps and look down but never called. Then he'd go to "their" chair to sleep – perhaps to dream they were together again.

Then one fall day he went out and we never saw him again. He, too, may have been some hunter's "game," but we never found his body. He was not on the road – though we searched everywhere. Perhaps the hardest part is losing a pet and not knowing what happened to them. If you know, at least you have closure.

Tinker and Lucky gazing out the window

JUNE WIEHE

Me holding "Frosty"

Frosty

Chapter Four

After losing Tinker, a friend had a Siamese cat who had kittens. They were not purebred, but there was an all-white one we hoped might change for I've heard Siamese are born white. She had a slight smudge to her nose at first but that disappeared and it was soon apparent we had a white cat! We named her "Frosty" and she had the very vocal Siamese voice. She could talk up a storm!

Me holding Frosty as a kitten

She was feisty, but loving. Her one vice, if you could call it that, was that she loved to nip. It was her way of saying "I love you!" but it was not very nice when she lay purring on your lap and suddenly you'd get a nip on the arm. The vet told us to snip her nose with a finger when she did it and she'd soon stop. Well, we tried that! When she nipped, we'd snip her nose. So, she continued to nip – then she would close her eyes, flatten her ears, and wait for the punishment! She said she simply had to nip but she was willing to take the result! It was hysterical to see her expression. We'd have to laugh and, of course, we gave up and let her do her "loving" nips without anymore "snips" – but she always waited for it. Each time she nipped, she'd close her eyes and flatten her ears and wait! She knew she was not supposed to do it but she just could not resist!

Awhile after acquiring Frosty, another black kitten that someone had dumped wandered in. We named him "Smokey." They never became the pals that Tinker

Smokey

and Lucky had been, but they seemed to have an agreement when we had company. Frosty would stroll through the living room and go into the kitchen – and Smokey would then come strolling through from the kitchen. The double takes our guests would take the first time it happened was hilarious! They'd look hard and then ask, "I thought I saw a white cat – but now it's black!"

I had a ceramic business at the time and had turned our breakfast nook into a workroom. The

Frosty

table was at the window and I put a box on the end to raise it to the window. I put a soft cloth on it so the cats could lay and look out the window. It became Frosty's exclusive spot. Greenware is

Frosty in tree

extremely fragile but the table would be loaded with it and Frosty never broke a single piece. She could leap from the floor and walk across the table without disturbing a thing!

Frosty was a very precocious cat. As a kitten, her greatest pleasure was a large ball of yarn. She would tear around the house with it winding back and forth from one room to the next. The yarn would be caught around chair legs, table legs, and everything else until the ball was completely unwound and Frosty had an enormous web throughout the house. She always appeared extremely pleased with the result, especially watching me crawl around trying to undo her hard work!

Usually, as soon as she got the rolled up ball back, she would do the same thing again. How did she manage to do it? Get the end caught, then run and unroll it and get it wound tight? We were never able to determine. No other cat we ever had did that. They would just roll it about and play – never construct an intricate web! The only way to stop Frosty was to withhold the yarn ball, which we did, limiting her to one "web" a day!

She also had a fetish for opening doors! When Frosty was left alone, we could come home to find every cabinet door, closet door, and drawers pulled open! Nothing would be disturbed, but she just liked opening doors! She also knew which ones pushed and which ones pulled. The only thing that stopped her was a lock! Latched doors were no problem. She simply stretched her paws up and grasped the handle until it turned and unlatched! Then she'd hook her paw underneath the door and heave it open!

She always left us open-mouthed in amazement when we saw how she accomplished her feats of prowess! She was a powerful cat – no doubt from constantly working her muscles like that! She would heave and pull as long as it took to do what she wanted!

We tried shutting her in the kitchen but the push door was – can I say it? – a push over! We tried blocking it with a chair. No problem! If it won't push; pull! Being afraid she'd squash herself doing that; we gave up and resigned ourselves to closing everything when we got home!

We never allowed any of our cats to get on tables or counters, so Frosty's openings were always what she could reach from the floor. One thing that happened when she was still a young kitten may have enforced that trait in her.

We had beautiful built-in corner cabinets in the dining room. On the bottom of one shelf, Mother had a collection of salt and pepper shakers. Frosty jumped up one day and happened to knock over a pepper shaker. She put her nose down into it and began to sneeze so much we were afraid she'd run out of breath and die! "Ah choo! Ah choo! Ah choo!" She sneezed as fast as she could to get the pepper out! When the paroxysm ended she was a subdued little kitten who never made that mistake again!

Frosty sometimes led Smokey astray. She could get into places but always knew how to get out. Not so with Smokey. He'd follow Frosty into something and soon we'd hear him crying and find him in a crawl space or in a mess of boxes where he could not find an exit.

Frosty on roof - Queen of all she surveys

One day a window left open allowed Frosty to lead him up on the roof. Frosty came back in no trouble but all the calling and coaxing in the world could not get Smokey to come back to the window. Dad had to get a ladder and go up on the roof to rescue him! Frosty loved the roof and would sit on top of the chimney like queen of the world, but we never let Smokey follow her there anymore!

JUNE WIEHE

Wags
(Pastel by June)

Chapter Five

One day a young dog was sitting on our terrace - a Heinz 57 variety - but the moment I saw him I said, "That's one mutt I could love!"

And, so, "Wags"* joined our family - a dog whose intelligence was unbelievable! He greeted the cats as friends but Frosty batted his nose. Smokey was another matter – he took to Wags as a duck takes to water. They became best friends.

Perhaps the strange thing about our doings with animals is the fact we never thought about their not getting along. I hear now they should be introduced gradually and never be left alone together at first. We just brought Wags into the house and told him, "Here's Frosty, and this is Smokey. They belong here. You want to join them?" Of course, it wasn't that casual. We held onto him while we introduced the cats, but he showed no aggression. So we let them get acquainted on their own.

* Sadly, many beautiful pictures of Wags are missing.

Wags quickly learned to leave Frosty alone because if he got too close, she'd slap his nose. But Smokey was a different colored cat! Those two played and slept together. Frosty was the outcast – living up to her name.

One morning after breakfast, I saw Frosty dragging herself along and discovered she was apparently paralyzed in her hind legs. She had eaten breakfast and seemed fine so we were shocked and dumbfounded, wondering what on earth could have caused it. We bundled her in a blanket and Mother and Dad drove her to the vet.

Mother had put heavy gloves on, but before they could reach the vet, Frosty died, and in her death throes bit mother badly right through the glove. They brought her home and Daddy buried her while Mother went to the doctor for her bite. He treated it and then said that we would need to get Frosty tested for rabies. We knew she didn't have rabies, but Dad dug her up and we took her to the vet for an autopsy while her head was sent off to be tested for rabies. The vet could find nothing wrong and could only conclude she had died of acute indigestion! I have always wondered just what happened to bring such a sudden change in that six-year-old cat. Acute indigestion did not sound very credible. P. S. No rabies either!

Neither Wags nor Smokey missed Frosty. Life went on as usual for them. Wags was a favorite of all the children in the neighborhood and they'd come to the door to ask, "Can Wags come out and play?" Of course, Wags was delighted to do so! I wonder how many childless households with a dog have neighborhood children come to the door just to ask if the dog can come out and play? Whenever a kid passed on a bike or on foot, and Wags was out, we would hear, "Hiya, Wagsy!"

My walks through the field and woods in back were a never-ending pleasure. I loved hiding from Wags and watching him work out

Me with Wags

the trail. All I had to do was tell him to "Stay" and then I would try to mess up my trail until I got somewhere to see him work it out. I would whistle and he'd go to his nose until he found me.

Training Wags

Wags was perfectly behaved. When I gave a command like, "Sit," "Stay," or "Lie down," it was followed instantly. There would not be a move until I said, "Okay!" I mean Wags never, ever made a wrong move, and every command and trick I taught him was learned the very first time! When I taught him "Sit," I said the word and put him in his position. Then I patted and praised him, telling him what a good dog he was. Then he got up and danced around so happy I was pleased. I said "Sit!" and he instantly sat down and got the same lavish praise.

No treats, nothing to eat, just praise. He had the command. From that moment on when I told him to sit – he sat!

It was the same with everything else I taught him. Show him once what I wanted and he had it! Besides all the usual "dog" commands, there were tricks - all learned the same quick, easy way. Wags' only limitation was my inability to convey what I wanted. He rolled over, he said his prayers, he played dead, and he walked on a tightrope (two clothes poles resting on supports). Of course, sitting up and shaking paws were very simple.

The trick that guests always marveled at was when I would put a tempting piece of meat in front of him after the command, "Sit, stay," and then saying, "Don't touch it!" I would leave the room for an extended period and he would sit and wait until I returned and say, "Okay!" Not until then would he snatch it up and eat it! The fact that he would obey and continue to obey on command, even when I was not in sight, never ceased to amaze people.

One day on our walk, I saw him pick up and eat something when he was half a field away.

It made him very sick. As soon as he was well, I took an old bicycle tire we used to played tug of war with. It was one of his favorite games and he usually won! This time when we were tugging away, I had the end of his leash in my hand; it was not attached to his collar. I said, "Drop it!" Of course he had no idea what that meant, so I said it again and slapped his nose with the leash. He dropped the tire in surprise and I praised and petted him. We began the game again and when we were going good, I said, "Drop it." Wags dropped it like a hot potato! That's all it took. From then on, when he was a distance from me, and if I'd see him pick up something, I'd yell, "Drop it!" Then I would say, "Don't touch it!" and he'd sit and wait until I got to him to see what it was. If it were something he could have, I'd only have to say, "Okay" – if not, we'd go on our way. It was a great relief to me to have that kind of control.

There was only one thing I couldn't stop him at. If I saw a squirrel or deer before he started to run after it, I could order him to "Stay" and he would. But if he had already started to run, I could not stop him.

One day, however, a big buck changed Wag's mind. We were in the woods about a mile from home. He ran over the crest of a hill in front of us and I heard a sudden yelp. Wags came flying back over the hill with a big buck hot on his tail!

Wags ran to me and crowded against my legs. I put the leash on him, though at that point it was not needed (superfluous) - he was not going to get away from my legs! It would have been funny if I hadn't been so afraid, because Wags refused to look at the deer. It was as if he was saying – "If you don't see him, he's not there!"

That buck was so mad! He shook his antlers at me – and he had a huge rack – then he pawed at the ground and charged! He ran past me about five feet away with that bark they have. He stopped ten feet away, again shaking his head and pawing the ground, before he charged past again – trying to lure the dog away from me.

Wags pressed tight to my legs with his back to the buck, desperately trying to pretend this was not happening. The buck charged several more times, getting a little closer each time, so I decided to try and make tracks!

A large tree ten feet away looked more promising than the sapling I was trying to keep between the deer and me. Cautiously, Wags and I made our way to the bigger tree. When we stopped, the charging started again. We seemed to be at an impasse. That buck was not about to stop his harassment, so we started to walk slowly from tree to tree - Wags hugging my legs so tight I could hardly walk. When the buck stopped charging and just started following, I became more confident and kept walking at a steady pace towards home.

Do you know that buck followed us the whole mile home? He would occasionally let out that barking snort as if to urge us to move faster. Not once did Wags turn his head to see the deer! As we approached our back road, the buck dropped further behind and we reached home safely. I was thankful he'd been too afraid to attack me, but he sure wanted to murder poor Wags! Wags never chased a deer again!

Wags was such a friendly dog. I never thought of him as a protector, but one day he showed his true worth. We were on our way home from our usual walk when Wags suddenly swung back against my legs, stopping me in my tracks with a low growl. Never in his life had he done anything like that before, especially never a growl.

He then bounced forward on stiff legs, barking his head off at a clump of bushes. I could see nothing and I tried to calm him down with my voice but he was hysterical and his look at me was a desperate, "Don't come any nearer!" It was such a departure from his usual behavior that I just stood there and talked to him asking what was wrong while he still kept barking at the bushes – jumping up and down on stiff legs!

I don't know how long it lasted – it seemed long at the time - but suddenly a man rose out of that clump of bushes! It was the last thing I expected to see. My mind had been on something like a snake! Maybe you could call him a snake in the bushes! I asked, "What are you doing there?" He did not say a word, but just walked off into the woods!

The man may not have had any evil intentions, but I was so proud of Wags, I could hardly contain myself! I knew that I had a definite

Mother with Wags on a blanket

defender and protector! Fortunately, that was the only time Wags had to act like that.

When I say he was exceptional; he was. He loved lying partially on laps at night on the couch. Because he had a lot of white hair (which he shed) we put down a blanket. We never covered the couch when it wasn't in use because Wags would never get on it. People said he would when left alone, but he never did because there was never a white hair to be found.

He adored toys and we kept them on a low shelf on the mangle in the kitchen. He knew what every toy was. We could say, "Bring your shoe," and he'd get his shoe. Whatever we asked for, he'd bring! He also had a strong sense of what was his and what was ours! My garden shoes were worse than some of those we gave him to play with, but I could kick them off in the middle of the floor just before we all left the house and they would never be touched.

Christmas was the best time. Wags knew Christmas meant gifts as well as any kid, and he could hardly wait after the tree was put up. We wrapped all his gifts in lots of newspaper because he loved to rip them open.

On Christmas Eve, all the gifts would go under the tree, Wags' and Smokey's, as well. Wags would delight in checking them all out, almost as if he was counting how many he had. Smokey knew which were his because he could smell the catnip, I think.

We would go to bed, never worrying that the gifts would be disturbed, because they never were. Christmas morning we always had breakfast first, then came present opening. Wags knew his gift was inside the newspaper and he would make short work of getting to the prize. He'd nose the gift as if to say, "Oh boy!" Then he ran to us for another one! By the time all the presents were opened, the floor was a mass of torn paper, and exhausted Wags would be stretched out in the middle! Christmas was always a ball when we had Wags. He was as "kid-like" as a dog could be.

Wags' vocabulary was phenomenal. I gave up after counting 250 words and phrases. Volume or tones of voice had nothing to do with it. I could whisper a command or yell it like I was furious — he'd always respond correctly. He was so smart!

We watched the circus on TV back then, and there were a lot of dog acts. Each dog would have a one- or two-trick specialty. Wags could do them all! I'd see a new trick and have to teach it to Wags, so he was a circus dog all by himself! Never was an animal more willing to try anything I asked! Jumping through hoops or over sticks, catching objects in midair; simple!

One day Smokey and Wags cornered a mouse under the shelving of ceramic paints under the work table. For a while they just sat and watched expectantly. Smokey had cat patience but Wags had to make things happen. He jumped up with a bark that said, "The heck with this! Let's go get him!"

In a second, bottles were flying in every direction as he tried to get at the mouse. Smokey was so busy dodging bottles that, of course, the mouse got away!

The looks Smokey gave Wags after that spoke volumes. "Dummkopf! We could have caught him but for you!" Of course, I was the one who had to clean up the mess and put things to right!

Because of the highway, we had a hundred foot line to hook Wags' collar to when we let him out alone. I tried to find a harness because I was always afraid of him breaking his neck when he'd hit the end of the line so hard. Unfortunately, I could never find a harness that fit him.

My fears came true. One day he hit into the line so hard, he dislocated a vertebra in his neck. The vets said nothing could be done and we had to have him put to sleep. Losing Wags hit me so hard I was sick for many weeks after. He was only six years old.

Smokey grieved for Wags so badly, we were afraid we'd lose him but he gradually got over it.

Mother and Cindy

Cindy enjoying the snow

Chapter Six

The winter after we lost Wags, Mother (pictured on left) went to get the car out of the garage and found a huge German Shepherd curled up on a bag of tire chains. She was skin and bones. So, of course, mother brought her into the kitchen. The next thing that happened, I still can't believe. Smokey came flying into the kitchen – right up to that huge dog that was twice the size Wags had been – and began weaving in and out of her legs, purring like an outboard motor! You could see the dog's first instinct was to grab that cat, but she quickly realized she was the imposter and she'd better behave herself!

Her size made no difference to Smokey. He loved that dog the moment he saw her. He had absolutely no fear of her and did his best to make her welcome! She was smart enough to recognize that, and from that moment on they were the best of pals! Another painless joining!

Cindy

We took her to the vet who estimated her age at twelve, and said that she was one of the finest specimens of Shepherds he'd ever seen. He was sure she'd been a champion in her day. When she fattened up and had a bath, she was gorgeous. We looked on her as a Cinderella, so we named her "Cindy" for short.

Smokey was the happiest cat to have another dog companion and Cindy seemed to be just as happy – but one thing became absolutely clear - she was my dog! She loved Mother and Dad, but made me her responsibility.

If I so much as got up to change channels on the TV – she'd get up with me. I'd have to say, "Stay, Cindy" every time I moved to keep her settled! It reached the point I had to take her with me wherever I went because if I didn't, Mother said all she did was pace and cry until I got back!

If anyone came to the door, she'd sound off in a most vicious way. But the instant I said, "Okay, Cindy," she was all wags and friendly. After that first greeting, though, most people were hesitant to touch her!

One day the UPS man came to the door and got that thunderous greeting. He looked down at his pad, back at her, and then asked, "That's a small, friendly dog?" I laughed and said, "She's a new one!" He scratched out the note and spoke the words he wrote down, "Big, unfriendly dog!"

I made a collar for her of quarter-inch elastic to attach her tag, as Cindy needed no leash whatsoever. What I said was the law to Cindy. I could not stop Wags when he started to run after something, but Cindy would stop on a dime when I called her. But I got many a comment over that quarter-inch elastic collar!

Cindy could not manage stairs, so she slept in the dining room on a large bed we had made for her. (She needed a large one!) As I said before, she made me her responsibility and was on constant alert by me all day. The moment I moved, she was on her feet ready to accompany me, and the only way I could prevent that was to say, "Stay, Cindy!" Saying that became a regular habit. When bedtime came, Cindy (being an old dog) was exhausted by her constant vigilance and alertness. When I showed her to her bed and said, "Good night, Cindy," she finally relaxed.

It was so funny. If, for any reason, any of us had to go downstairs overnight, Cindy never heard a thing! She'd be dead to the world snoring away! A burglar could have walked away with the house at night!

Come morning, she'd stand at the bottom of the stairs and "talk" a blue streak telling me all about her night. She never barked, she just made all sorts of sounds trying her best to communicate. Of course, I'd say, "Is that so? You don't say so!" I wish I'd had a recorder to tape her "talks."

When I'd visit neighbors, I had to take her

along and would leave her outside the door – just telling her to "stay." She'd lay down and never say a word or make a fuss no matter how long the visit. She never left that spot until I came out and we went home. Although it

Cindy playing with neighbor's puppy

was hard for her to get in and out, when I went out in the car, she had to go along. She took up the whole back seat but she never made a fuss no matter how long I left her. She evidently did not feel the need to have to go with me and be at my side continually unless we were home!

We had her two wonderful years before her hind legs finally gave out. One morning she could not get up so we had to have the vet come to the house to put her to sleep.

For many weeks after her demise, I'd catch myself going to say, "Stay, Cindy," every time I moved because it had became so much of a habit. That fact only emphasized her absence. Smokey, of course, was again traumatized by the loss of another dog pal.

JUNE WIEHE

Smokey trying to open door like Frosty

Chapter Seven

Shortly after losing Cindy we moved from New Jersey to Virginia. It was a seven-hour trip by car so Dad made a huge crate for Smokey, but he yelled and struggled to get out. Once out he gave his paw to Dad to hold and was fine. Smokey had never been a lap cat, but on this journey he didn't want a lap either. He only wanted someone to hold his paw!

We had 2.7 acres with nothing but woods around us. In New Jersey, the trees in the yard were large with big limbs starting seven-to-eight feet up from the ground that Smokey had loved to climb. Here, the trees were tall and skinny with limbs not starting for twenty feet! It was so comical to watch Smokey. He would go to each tree circling it and

Smokey

looking up as if to say, "What kind of tree is this? Where are the limbs?" He never attempted to climb them, he'd just circle them, looking up in disbelief.

Freddie the Freeloader drinking from pail

Another black cat wandered in shortly after. He had bad breathing problems so we did not let him with Smokey but let him in the cellar at night and during bad weather. One of my girlfriends came for a visit and dubbed him "Freddie the Freeloader" and the name stuck. Then another black kitten appeared that we called "Chipper" because he was so vivacious. He and Freddie became close friends until winter set in and Freddie's breathing problems became so

Chipper

bad that the vet said he should be put to sleep.

Chipper was devastated by the loss of Freddie and shortly thereafter disappeared. I will always believe he went looking for Freddie. Smokey remained.

Several years after moving to Virginia, the woman Smokey had been so fond of in New Jersey came for a visit. Well! You never saw such a greeting, and Smokey was so overjoyed that while she was here, he became a lap cat for the first time in his life. Every time she sat down, Smokey would get on her lap! After she left, he never sat on a lap again!

Cindy with Smokey

Father and Flash

Chapter Eight

Next on our doorstep was a female Pointer. She had been badly abused and it took us two days before we could touch her. She was too wild to bring into the house and she was about the fastest thing on four legs I'd seen. One second, she'd be in the front yard, next in the back! So, we named her "Flash." She became a loving dog but mostly an outdoor one. We'd put her in the cellar at night but she had free run of the yard during the day. She and Smokey became friends, but Flash was too busy to do more than touch noses on her way to something else!

She was a tremendous watchdog and made us feel extremely secure. One day, I was home alone when a car pulled in with four rather scruffy looking men in it. Flash did her usual thing of running as fast as she could get around the car, barking furiously. She would run so fast around a car that no one could get out of any door without

Flash

coming face to face with her. The men asked if she would bite and I said, "Yes," because I guessed she would the way she was acting! I did not try to stop her dashing, and the men who had asked if my horses were for sale, left after I said, "No."

Oh yes – you read right. By this time I had acquired two horses! When we moved to Virginia, there were people on the farm behind us whose mare had given birth to a beautiful colt they named "Thunder." Unfortunately, they moved away after that.

In the meantime, I had become acquainted with friends who had horses and would ride with them. All my life I'd wanted a horse of my own – so one day we learned the people who had Thunder wanted to sell him. He was now two years old, so those friends and I went to see the owners. They also had a mare for sale. We rode the horses. I rode Thunder and fell immediately in love. He was cheaper than the mare and my friend did not want to pay extra but liked the mare. I told her I'd pay the

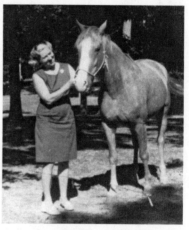

difference if she would give me one breeding to an Arabian stallion. She agreed.

For a number of years, I had been spending two months out of the year out in Colorado on an

Me with Thunder

Arabian horse ranch and loved the breed. Isn't it strange how things come about?

I boarded Thunder with my friends until I could build a stable and make a fenced pasture. At the time of the sale, no one knew the mare "Calico" was already pregnant by Thunder! So, we had to wait until the following year when a beautiful, snow white filly was born. After that, I had Calico bred to a Raffles bred Arabian stallion. The following spring, I had a beautiful half-Arabian filly I named "Melodee." She always looked like a purebred.

Mother and Melodee

Me training Melodee on lunge line

Anyway, those were the horses the men asked about. To this day, I don't believe that was what they stopped by for, but I'll never know. I do know that Flash got rid of them in a hurry by her threats!

When Flash came in heat we kept her penned but a neighbor's beautiful collie got to her for only a few seconds before we stopped him – that was all the time he needed.

When Flash began having puppies, we had the vet come because she did not seem well. He gave her a shot because she was low in some nutrient. She had nine puppies and the vet said she would not be able to nurse that many. So he put six females to sleep, leaving her with three males. Half an hour later, I went into the

Flash feeding pups

cellar to check on her and did a double take – I counted bodies and there were four! She'd had another pup! A half hour after that, I went down and counted five! By that time, I was afraid that I'd find a new pup every time I went down! Fortunately that was it!

Flash was spotted-brown and white. Her pups had more Collie in them with longer hair and fringed tails. They were all black with white collars, noses, paws, and bellies and white tips on their tails. By six weeks of age, they could all "shake paw," and "sit up" and beg.

Three times a day we took a walk through the woods and all I kept doing was counting, "One, two, three, four, five!" I had to make sure I

Top to bottom - Teddy, Pal, Buddy, King and Blaze

kept track of all five and didn't lose one along the way! They were good pups, however, and never wandered off. I had them all named and they knew their names - Buddy, Pal, Teddy, Blaze, and King.

For some reason, Teddy was the jinxed one. If a tail got stepped on – it was Teddy's. If one got in a spot they couldn't get out of – it was Teddy. If one got stung by a bee – it was Teddy! He was the hard luck pup from the beginning. Then one day I saw Flash and the puppies flying back from the front road. Flash never, ever went near the road. I don't know if the pups had wandered up and she went after them, but there were only four pups with her.

With a sinking heart, I went out to the road and there lay dear little Teddy. The dark star he'd apparently been born under, ended his very brief life at eleven weeks of age.

Whether the other pups knew what happened, I don't know, but they never went near the road again. Blaze and King went to a new home at thirteen weeks but Buddy and Pal became part of our family.

Pal grew to be a big dog while Buddy was more compact. Buddy was the courageous one while Pal was a big baby. If Pal had a hurt paw there was no way he could walk on three legs! He'd hobble and cry, and beg for sympathy and you could almost see Buddy and Flash look at him in disgust!

One day after one of our walks through the

Sandy and Pal

woods, Buddy and Pal came back with a tan puppy! I have no idea where they found him but they were so delighted. They crowded him up to me as if to say, "Can we keep him, Mom? Can we keep him?"

The puppy, fully weaned, was adorable – a golden lab cross and he followed happily along to home! No one ever claimed him and no one reported a missing puppy so we assumed, like too many others, he was simply dumped off. So, "Sandy" became a part of the family.

Unlike the others who were all forgivers, if you accidentally stepped on a tail or something,

Me with Sandy and Flash

Sandy was not! Hurt Sandy some way and go up to say how sorry you were and you'd be met with bared teeth and threatening growls. It was really so comical we'd have to laugh and try and placate him with, "Oh Sandy, I'm so sorry!" It never worked. It was at least a half hour before he'd relent and let us pet him again!

Sandy

Flash and Buddy

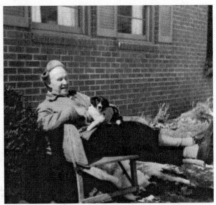

Dad holding King

Buddy playing in water

Pal and I playing tug of war

Smokey with Flash and pups

Me with Buddy and Pal

Chapter Nine

Shortly after the pups were born, we lost Smokey. He was eighteen years old. He proved to be the second longest survivor of all our pets with the exception of the horses. Needless to say – we really missed that cat!

One day when the four dogs and I were taking our usual walk, we met a pack of what looked like feral dogs led by a large wolfish looking black dog. Pal, Flash, and Sandy took off in high gear – running away, but dear brave Buddy planted himself in front of me.

I was scared to death because there were five big menacing dogs and only my smallest was facing them. I was so afraid I was going to see him torn to pieces in front of my eyes!

When the leader bared his teeth with a threatening growling snarl and they started towards us (they were already within five feet of us), Buddy gave a ferocious growl of his own and leaped for the leader! I mean he gave a charge that meant business, as if to say, "Don't you dare growl at my mistress!" To my immense relief, instead of the uneven brawl I'd feared, the five turned tail and fled with Buddy barking and growling behind them speeding them on their way!

He pranced back to me with a laughing face and wagging tail and I could imagine him saying, "What were you worried about Mom? You knew I'd protect you! They couldn't bully me!" You can imagine the love and attention I bestowed on him then!

As soon as the danger passed, the other three dogs came running back to get chewed out by me! "A fine lot of cowards you are!" I accused, "Leaving Buddy to face that pack alone!" After that I always carried a walking stick with me, as I had not had a thing to even help Buddy if he'd needed it.

Another time when we were walking I heard one of the dogs yelp as they all came running back to me – Flash on three legs. We got home and called the vet. He said as he was coming he was trying to think what could have happened so fast and thought, "snake bite." That proved to be the case. He thought it had probably been a copperhead. By the time he got here, Flash's shoulder was swelled way up. He gave her a shot and medicine for us to give her. She was one sick dog for a while but pulled through.

It seemed like it was the walks when things happened – fortunately, not too often. One spring, Buddy disappeared on our morning walk. He never responded to my whistle and calls which was something that never happened. All the dogs always came when called.

Every time we went out the other dogs would disappear into a thicket of brambles and poison ivy. I figured they were going to Buddy's body. I had never heard a bark or yelp when he disappeared which was so puzzling to me. I kept watching for buzzards but never saw any, which also made me wonder.

Seventeen days after disappearing – the other dogs and I had just gotten home when I looked with unbelieving eyes. Buddy came out from the trail hardly able to walk! His hind legs had obviously been paralyzed for a while but he was coming as fast as he could – skin and bones but so happy to be home.

In examining him, we came to the conclusion (right or wrong) that he had come upon a doe with a fawn and she had hit him before he could even bark and knocked him out. Even after seventeen days, he still had a big lump on the top of his head. Then she'd battered his back for there were hoof marks all down his spine.

We guess he had been paralyzed because he was still almost dragging his hind legs. We guessed it had happened near the stream where he would drag himself and he lived on water alone for seventeen days. Once he got food and love again he recovered rapidly as he was only two years old.

However, from that time on, every time winter rolled around he would hurt. Maybe the battering on his back had caused permanent damage – possibly a form of arthritis. Anyway when he'd first get up he would whimper and cry in pain – then in defiance of it he would begin to run as hard as he could to work it out! I'd heard alfalfa pills were good for arthritis so I'd give him four tablets a day of the alfalfa and he had no more trouble. He never seemed to suffer in warm weather but as soon as it got cold I'd have to start the alfalfa pills again and he'd be fine.

Though Sandy was the youngest he was the first of the dogs to go. He developed a brain tumor and had to be put to sleep. Shortly after that, Flash got cancer and we lost her.

Buddy lived for twelve years. One day we noticed he was bleeding a little from the mouth and took him to the vet who could find nothing wrong – said to feed him on soft food. Buddy was always a happy-go-lucky dog – never a worrier like his brother Pal was.

After getting him home as I was petting and loving him, I noticed that in the black spot he had on his white chest was a tiny hole. I called the vet and asked if he could have been shot by perhaps a BB or something. He was skeptical but I was afraid the wound had penetrated to his throat and that's why he was bleeding.

It didn't seem to bother him; he ate and played as usual. Then a few days later he took off across the yard in a purposeful manner. I asked him where he thought he was going and he gave me that laughing look of his and kept going. When he didn't come home I started calling around and learned a neighbor's Saint Bernard had come into heat and jumped out the window and went off with Buddy.

After several days the Saint Bernard went home but Buddy didn't. Buzzards helped us find him. I can only think the activity he'd done had caused whatever his wound was to prove fatal.

Pal, grieving his brother's loss became a house dog. He was such a big baby! He could not stand thunderstorms and had to sit with his head in your lap drooling away. Unfortunately that year we had a lot of storms and I spent hours trying to comfort him. Many a night I sat up with him because most of the storms seemed to come around 2AM!

He was much too big to sit in a lap but that's what he wanted to do! So he'd sit between my legs, facing me, often with one paw on my leg – panting so hard I had to keep a towel on my lap and would still get soaked!

Tommy, Cricket and Jack

Chapter Ten

Pal lived only a year after Buddy and suddenly we were without any dogs at all! – but not without any cats!!

Two feral cats came for handouts. The female was a gorgeous pale calico, the male a black and white with a bobbed tail. We called him "Shorty," the female was always just "Mama Cat."

They showed up shortly after Flash arrived. While they never became close buddies there were never any confrontations. They all got along just fine. Come spring, of course, and Flash got pregnant and so did Mama Cat. She had her kittens in the planter on the porch. Five beautiful babies, two tigers, one black, one tortoise shell and one long haired orange.

JUNE WIEHE

A few days later they disappeared! I guessed it was because I'd handled them. The problem with Mama Cat was she'd sit beside you, take walks with you, but just don't attempt to touch her! A touch would make her leap as if she'd been hit with a red hot poker!

Though she'd come for her food, I never found where she'd hid her babies. By the time I discovered they were under the tool shed, they were wild. I began putting a large plate of food down outside their den. After I got far enough away, they'd come out and eat but dash away if I attempted to come nearer.

I was patient. Day by day I moved the plate farther from the den and closer to myself. I was finally able to stay while they ate and gradually I began to stroke them as they ate.

I finally got them up on the back stoop to eat, then one day I opened the kitchen door and put the food inside. The kittens came in but Mama Cat stayed out. When they were inside, we closed the door and after they were through eating we began to play with them. They were skeptical at first but being kittens were curious. I sat on the floor and cuddled them one by one then played with a string.

An hour was all it took. From then neither the home nor I were scary to them. They'd come in and eat and play – then go out with Mama Cat.

Shorty was the babysitter. I've heard tom cats will often kill kittens, but it was a joy to see him come strolling in with the kittens running out to meet him, tumbling all over him. The family would play together for a while, the two older cats acting as silly as the kittens. Then Mama Cat would go off and let Shorty to care for the kittens!

The tortoise shell and long haired orange kitten were females, and I named the orange one "Rusty" and the other had such a funny marking on her face that I called her "Valentine" after the song. The black one was "Cricket." The larger, lighter tiger stripe was "Tommy" and the smaller one became "Jack" – for jumping! He was the best leaper I ever saw. He'd leap to the kitchen window sill from the ground outside – a jump of six feet, as if it were nothing.

Jack was also a champion climber. He'd

Cricket

Valentine

Jack

Sweetie Pie

follow the squirrels up the trees and follow them out to the tip of the limbs. One time he looked like he was going to try and leap to the next tree after the squirrel until my frantic calls brought him back down the normal way!

He was my shadow and followed me everywhere. His favorite method of coming in was leaping to a window for us to open so he could come in.

One day I saw the kittens come flying back from the front road – but one was missing. I went up and found dear, little Rusty had been killed.

While I was still trying to tame the kittens, another one showed up – a semi-long haired female as sassy as they come. That's what I should have named her, but in attempt to change her nature I named her "Sweetie Pie!" She was a gorgeous fluffy orange who always maintained her long hair perfectly. She also was the primadonna of the cat world. "She wanted to be alone!" While friendly she held herself aloof because – of course – she was the beautiful aristocrat while they were merely short-haired "alley cats!"

Sometime between the time he was born and we finally found the kittens again, Cricket had damaged one eye. The first thing we had to do was take him to a vet who removed the eye. Having only one eye never slowed Cricket down. He was the clown of the bunch and a very loving lap cat.

One thing he did was hilarious and gave us all belly laughs every night because it was so funny. Mother sat on one side of the couch and I on the other. Cricket would start the evening on Mother's lap then want to switch to mine. I'd say, "Cricket, I don't want you – stay there!" He'd stop and settle back, then he'd begin his ploy. I'd pretend not to see him as one foot moved ever so slowly forward. Then the next foot, as slow as possible, would move forward. If we had captured it on video, you would have sworn we shot it in slow motion - super slow motion at that! Step by increment step, Cricket transversed the middle part of the couch until one foot was planted on my lap. Then slowly the rest of him, very gently and quietly, settled in! Trying to contain the laughter he was giving us with this antic was the hardest! When

I'd hug him and say it was okay, he'd heave a big sigh and relax – his mission accomplished.

This occurred every night because, of course, he was always rewarded with my lap - which was exactly what he wanted in the first place! He just figured out a unique way to do it!

Jack was my shadow. He was always near me and if outside and me inside, he'd leap to a window sill because he knew I'd always open it to let him in.

Valentine was a very loving cat. The only cat I've ever owned who'd came running when she heard the vacuum cleaner! The noise never frightened her and one time when I had the attachment on – I brushed her with it. The suction pulled out all her loose hair and she adored the feel of it! After that she insisted on being vacuumed every time it was used – while all the other cats disappeared.

All the cats loved to take walks with us. They'd follow us through the woods never running off but all trotting along in high spirits – just as our dogs had. They actually stayed close where the dogs would range farther.

One day Tommy disappeared and we never saw him again. We searched the woods and roads and watched for buzzards and spread the word but Tommy was gone for good. We of course had all the kittens neutered.

The first day of hunting season, Jack disappeared. His vanishing was a real puzzlement because he was such a home body. I'm not sure if he became some hunter's game or if he had maybe followed a squirrel up a tree and tried to jump to another tree limb and fell – but again there were no tell-tale buzzards or any body on the road to bury. Shorty had also disappeared. That's the big disadvantage of allowing cats to go outside. You rarely learn what happens to them when they just disappear.

When Mama Cat became pregnant again, we took her to the SPCA, as we knew we could not deal with more kittens – providing we'd be able to find them before they became too wild to tame or rather to catch!

As usual another kitten soon wandered in! I think our house is marked "For strays – welcome!" This was another orange striped kitten that turned

Sammy

up in spring. He was a real character, always getting into mischief and insisting on helping you no matter what you were doing. We named him "Sammy." As fast as I planted onions – he dug them up! It was a great game for him! I had to keep redoing what he undone! Sammy made himself felt in every way. He lived his life to the hilt. The other cats had lost their kitten ways by now and were not so playful. Sammy on the other hand, lived to play and did it whole hardily. It seemed like he was trying to get a lifetime in as short a time as possible. He was the life of the party, so to speak.

Anyway, one day when he didn't come to my call, I went up on the road (which was always the first place I looked when one of the pets went missing.) Sammy had been hit by a car and lay dead. I picked him up and carried him back and Mother met me and took him into her arms and said, "The joy has gone out of our lives!"

Another heartbreak was soon to follow. Cricket, who never went out front, met his doom under the wheels of another car. The irony was that at that time there was hardly a car on the road. Yet they had to pass just at the time our pets had.

We were then down to Valentine and Sweetie Pie. But as usual – not for long!

Mother and Fritz

Chapter Eleven

One day when Mother, Dad, and I, and the two cats were in the front yard up from the road strutted a half grown orange striped cat – tail straight up – self assurance all apparent. He went up to Valentine and got slapped down. He didn't retaliate but shook himself off and went up to Sweetie Pie with the same result – a spitting hiss and slap to the face. He came over to each of us weaving between our legs saying in unmistakable fashion, "I'm home!"

And home he was – though for weeks we threatened him with the SPCA! He was indomitable! The naughtiest cat we'd ever had! We called him "Snickle-Fritz" because he was into everything! He didn't know how to walk on the floor and he refused to acknowledge "No" as part of his vocabulary! Every time he went up to the other cats they would knock him silly, and it suddenly dawned on us that not once did Fritz retaliate.

One night, shortly after his arrival, he insisted on lying on top of the TV. I'd get up and put him down with a firm, "No, Fritz!" He would wait until I sat down and get up on it again with the same result. After a dozen times I gave up and told him, "Okay, get radiated if you want to!"

He looked at me with bright eyes, jumped down and came over and got on my lap! Purring like an outboard motor! He'd finally got us to understand what he was about! I know you are going to doubt what you read about this amazing cat, but it's all true.

Fritz was a cat filled with so much love that

he could not understand why everyone – including other animals could not love him. Not one hiss or grumble ever came out of him. I had him thirteen years and never had one bite or scratch! Valentine and Sweetie Pie never got anything but persistent love until after a week they accepted him and Valentine and he became grooming buddies.

He did love to tease me though. He'd come and look at me with a real bright twinkle in his eye as if to say, "I'm going to do something naughty now – What are you going to do about it?" Then he'd start to scratch the rug or something he knew he was not supposed to do – all the while watching us with absolute laughter in his expression. Of course we'd yell at him and he'd take off in high gear – symbolically laughing all the way, I'm sure!

This was just a fun game and he know we knew it because once we accepted what he was he became a regular, well behaved cat. The only time he pretended to "misbehave" was when he told us he was – because he wanted to hear us yell and chase after him!

I could do anything in the world with him – even trim his toenails – something I've never been able to do with any other cat. One time he had a urinary infection and I had to give him an antibiotic pill every day for ten days.

No problem! Before breakfast I'd open his mouth and put in the pill – then give him his breakfast. There was never a struggle. He'd sit there and let me open his mouth – he didn't have to be held for it! The eleventh morning I gave him his breakfast and he just sat and looked at me. "Aren't you forgetting my pill?" he seemed to ask! He was actually looking forward to me opening his mouth and giving him his pill!

Apparently love emanated from him because nothing seemed afraid of him. The first time I saw him laying under the bird feeder with what I thought was an unsuspecting bird hopping around – I was ready to dash to its rescue but I noticed Fritz was showing no signs of lying in wait. He was just stretched out at leisure. Other birds came down and fed around him without fear. Somehow they know he was no threat. I tried to get pictures but the minute I came onto the scene, the birds would fly! Go figure!

One day Fritz was nose to nose with a fox! Friendliness on both sides! The same with raccoons and opossums! Never any aggression. Fritz simply could not understand that anyone could not love him!

He loved to converse with you. He'd sit and talk to you as long as you talked to him! Not just the ordinary meows – but all sorts of sounds. He really did his best to communicate. Oh! How I wished I understood what he was telling me! I pretended I did of course, but I'm sure he knew we were just passing some precious time together!

The other cats never cleaned their plates so Fritz did it for them! As a result he became a very big boy – a twenty-four pound Garfield in fact. Let me tell you – he was a lapful of a cat! And he always remained a lap cat.

Valentine was the next to go. She developed an inoperable tumor and had to be put to sleep. Fritz really missed her because they were always grooming each other.

During the next five years, I lost both of my parents, so Fritz, Sweetie Pie and I made a family.

Then one day I thought I heard a puppy bark on the porch. It turned out to be a tiny kitten with a most unusual voice! It would not let me get near, so I got some warm milk and sat it down and backed off. The kitten was skin and bones with very sparse hair. It was about the size of a six week old kitten, but actually turned out to be much older – it had just almost been starved to death.

The worst thing for me was that little thing smelled the milk and then ran away! I bought out canned cat food – same response! Next I tried cat kibble – the kitten refused to eat! It just kept crying. I put water out – and left all the food and milk out but the poor, starving kitten never touched a thing nor would it let me get near it. The following day it was still here – still not eating or drinking but by patient sitting and a lot of sweet talk I was finally able to get hold of her.

It was like holding a feather, she was so light. She was just skin stretched over bone! I locked her in the bathroom because she was so wild. I was afraid she'd find a hiding place and die before I could tame her. Since she refused everything – in desperation I cut up some raw beef kidney, and she dove in! Raw meat was what she wanted! Since Smokey had lived eighteen years on a diet of nothing but raw beef kidney, I knew it wouldn't hurt her. She still wouldn't touch anything else so I'd leave some water on the raw kidney, so she'd got more moisture. She lived in the bathroom for a week until she became more friendly and not so afraid. Fritz took over when I let her out. He

Fritz grooming Shadow

groomed her and loved her, but unlike Valentine, she never reciprocated. He'd put one ear down for her to lick but she ignored the plea – so Fritz finally realized he'd never get return favors from her but he never stopped taking care of her. Though a female, Sweetie Pie was no mother. She never offered any grooming or love to the kitten. She left that to Fritz.

I named her "Shadow" because she was black and trailed me around. She was so tiny at first I was so afraid of stepping on her or tripping over her and taking a fall myself but fortunately that never happened.

*Fritz loved to sleep on his back
and he and Shadow always slept together*

Actually her color is not really black because she has a light undercoat and stripes are visible on her legs and tail. The overall effect is motley because wherever the fur is separated, the light undercoat shows then, so sometimes I tell her she's moth-eaten! On her vet card, she's listed as blue-black!

Shadow turned Fritz into a kitten again. She'd pounce on him and they'd have a wrestling match. But they slept together all the time, as you can see by the pictures.

One thing I have to mention is that Fritz is the only cat I've ever had who liked to watch TV if birds or animals were involved. If something really interested him, he'd go sit in front of the TV.

Fritz watching TV

Sweetie Pie was the next to go. I had had her for sixteen years, so she had a good life. I missed her, but neither Fritz nor Shadow did.

Fritz, you might say, ate himself to death.

At the age of thirteen, his enlarged heart gave out and rather then watch that devil-may-care even loving cat slowly die on his own, I had him put to sleep. It's been twelve years and I still miss that sweet, mischievous cat!

Shadow's presence made the loss bearable. She's a totally different cat who has spoiled me for any other, So shy, no one has ever seen more than her tail going around a corner but the best behaved cat I've ever had.

Shadow

Above everything else, Shadow wants to be told she's a good cat! One correction is all she's ever needed. When she was still a half-green kitten, one day I was eating a sandwich on the dining room table when the phone rang. I went to answer it in the kitchen where the phone is. When I came back, Shadow was on the table eating my sandwich! I yelled and she took off in high gear. My words of horror and condemnation followed her.

"Don't ever let me catch you on that table again! That's a big NO-NO!"

Shadow cannot stand to be yelled at! For the rest of the day she kept her distance until I assured her she was really a good girl! She never got on the table again! I can leave food there with no worry whatever! One day she started to scratch the recliner and got the same horrified response from me. A number of times, since she doesn't know when I'm observing her, I've seen her raise a paw to that chair and then pause as though her brain kicks in to say, "That's a NO-NO!" She then lowers her paw and walks away! How do I know she doesn't do it when home alone? Not one pulled thread there or anywhere else!

When she began to go outside she wasn't sure she could come in again. She'd stand in front of the open door until I told her, "Oh what a good girl you are! Shadow's such a good girl!" In she comes happily because she's a good girl! It never failed!

Now there's no problem. She knocks and yells when she wants in! Sometimes, which is very rare, she doesn't answer my call right away – I bark like a dog and she comes flying!

Shadow

Hobo

Chapter Twelve

Another feral cat showed up one day. A beautiful, totally gray tom. He came only for food. If I was careful and quick, I could give him a quick stroke while he was eating but he'd swing a clawed paw at me if I tried too much! Like Mama Cat, he was totally feral. He got so he'd rub my legs but I mustn't try to touch him!

Sometimes he came morning and night. Sometimes he came only at night. He never stayed around in the day. When he first came, Shadow saw him through the window and let out a banshee yell like Kitty used to. I thought something terrible had happened to her until I saw the gray cat strolling by!

I called him "Hobo" because that's what he

was. One day I let Shadow out not seeing Hobo around. A few minutes later, I heard a cat fight. I ran to the door in time to hear Shadow's banshee yell again and to see Hobo heading for the tall timber!

Shadow flew in the door with all her fur standing on end. I went out and saw only Hobo's gray fur on the ground – so despite her smaller size she was the winner of that fight! I think it was the banshee yell that got him though.

Hobo never bothered the birds. He never stayed around after eating. In bad weather, hr stayed away but light rain never stopped him. The terrible winter of 2009 and 2010 was different. He was apparently snowed in somewhere. I didn't see him for weeks, then when he could finally navigate the snow he appeared. He was in good condition. He knew how to take care of himself. I had made him a nice bed on the porch but he never used it. There was also the barn with hay, but he never used that either.

Then after the weather changed, he never showed up for weeks. I thought perhaps he was "off on a toot" but after months passed, I guess

I've seen the last of Hobo. Another cat I'll never know what happened to.

Mittens was a black kitten with extra toes on his front feet – hence the name Mittens! He was only a brief transient. He just wandered off the same as he wandered in, or if something happened to him, I'll never know.

At this point, let me state it is black kittens that are often discarded like trash. Black cats are still apparently thought of as bad luck. That's why we acquired so many! But as I hope this book shows – one man's trash is another man's treasure. All the black cats I've had have been beautiful and highly intelligent. Loving, loyal companions! The horror stories we've all heard of puppies and kittens tossed out are beyond comprehension to me. How anyone can deliberately abandon a helpless animal makes me wonder about the human race. Such cruelty is heartbreaking. At least take them to the SPCA.

Shadow is still with me. She's fourteen years old, but she still plays like a kitten. We always start our morning with a high five. We don't "connect" because she's on the floor and I'm too high above her, but I raise my hand with my fingers spread and say, "Give me a high five!" She raises her right paw high with toes spread! Once in a while she'll refuse at first until I cajole a bit then the paw will come up and I'll tell her what a good girl she is!

She's a total lap cat. Every evening she can

Shadow moth-eater

hardly wait for me to finish dishes and sit down to watch TV. She trails me around crying until I sit down. She won't jump up – I have to lift her up with an "ups-a-daisy!" However, when she's on my lap, I can do nothing except pet and talk to her - at least until she gets in a deep sleep. Before then if I pick up a book or paper to read, she jumps off in a huff! Of course she's back begging within a few minutes!

When it's time for bed, I'll tell her, "Beddy bye time." If she's on my lap I transfer her to the couch. If not on my lap – when I say the magic words – she comes up talking to me to have me pick her up and put her "to bed." After locking up the house I'll walk past her and say, "Goodnight Shadow." She never fails to respond with a goodnight meow!

So that's the story of my many pet friends. A part of my heart died with each one, but life goes on and each one remains so special. No two are alike, any more than people are. Each one is a precious memory and the best thing about writing about them was the wonderful memories it dredges up. Yes, and tears too, in a renewed sense of loss – but many more happy memories.

I hope this book awakens people to the wonderful possibilities of abandoned animals. The love they return for the person who takes them in is boundless – worth more than all the gold in the world! And, yes, I am on a soapbox for those who cannot speak for themselves!

LaVergne, TN USA
06 April 2011
223116LV00002B/26/P